# Historical Computing Volume I: Programming in *BEGINNERS ALL-PURPOSE SYMBOLIC INSTRUCTION CODE*

BY

## DR. PETA TRIGGER Ph.D, Ed.D

**K B P**

**2 Emms Hill Barns**

**Hamsterley**

**County Durham**

**First published 2014**

**ISBN 9781495398964**

**PRINTED BY CREATESPACE**

https://www.createspace.com

# FOREWORD

*BASIC* as the acronym suggests, is a simple and easy computer language to learn and use. I have found it useful in developing quite complex mathematical programs in the early stages so that I can concentrate on rationale without at first having to contend also with nuances and subtleties of a more complicated programming environment. Having established a workable rationale in a bug-free program running in *BASIC*, it can be used as the basis for re-writing the code in a faster-executing, more versatile and more modern programming environment (as is done in Volume III of this series).

In this Volume I, the history, construction and use of early *BASIC* is described and a number of miscellaneous example programs are discussed and their outputs shown. Volume II is particularly concerned with the computerisation of the non-parametric statistical tests described in Siegel's 'Non-Parametric Statistics for the Behavioural Sciences' and some additional useful statistical procedures in *BASIC* programs. Volume III describes the development of matrix programs to invert matrices with complex elements, to solve higher order simultaneous equations and the development of programs to solve polynomial equations based on iterative, successive approximation, using *BASIC* and then in *Borland TurboC*. The final book in the series, Volume IV, details the use of Assembly language (ASM) programming to develop machine code programs called from *BASIC*.

# TABLE OF CONTENTS

## CHAPTER NUMBERS, HEADINGS AND PAGE NUMBERS

# DIAGRAMS

## HEADINGS & PAGE NUMBERS

# 1. HISTORY OF *BASIC*

*BASIC* was developed by Kemeney and Kurtz at the Dartmouth College, New Hampshire (USA) in 1964. This contained just a few keywords to enable the general user to do simple arithmetical tasks and a little printing. Their vision was to create an environment where computers were welcoming to everyone. Their mission was to bring the technology to a wide range of schools, colleges and businesses. Spreading to home computing, *BASIC* went on to become the most widely used computer language in the world.

Interestingly, the designers also wished it to be a stepping-stone for students onto learning more powerful languages such as FORTRAN. This is the approach of the present author who has used *BASIC* as a stepping stone in programming complex tasks in the harder to learn and use but more efficient 'C' language producing files directly executable in *Windows,* as described in Volume III of this series.

At the time of the original *BASIC*, computers were large and difficult to program 'mainframe' machines which received their input via a card reader fed with punched cards prepared by the user from his/her program. The stack of cards was placed in a queue behind other users' stacks waiting to read into the computer. The computer then compiled the instructions and executed them. This system, known as a 'batch' processing system which permitted only one job to run at a time, was very inconvenient because cards which could easily be stacked out sequence could cause an error in execution, and a bug in the program was not identified to the user until the print-out of the output was obtained after a delay. Then the program had to be debugged, the punched cards associated with the offending part of the program replaced and the new stack of punched cards placed in the queue behind other jobs awaiting compilation and execution by the computer once more. It could take a number of such cycles before the program succeeded in running as intended, as I found out to my chagrin when I took 'A London FORTRAN Course' at university in the early 1970's, and again as late as 1977 when I took a Module 22 course on SPSS- a Statistical Package for the Social Sciences at London University's Institute of Education.

Whilst developing *BASIC*, Kemeney and Kurtz worked on 'time-sharing' which would enable more than one program to run on computers at the same time by sharing the Central Processing Unit of the computer and memory, with each program in turn allocated processing time.

Time-sharing would also enable several users at keyboards to interact directly with computers, and this required a new, simple and efficient programming language. Time sharing became a reality one night in May 1964, when at 4 a.m. two of the duo's enthusiastic band of students succeeded in running two simple *BASIC* programs simultaneously on on the Dartmouth Time Sharing System (DTSS), a network of multiple simple terminals connected to a large computer, the GE 225 mainframe computer at Dartmouth.

HP-1000 Time Sharing Basic System TTY-33 Terminal  (In 1969, Gates and Allen began writing *BASIC* programs at Lakeside High School in Seattle using this same kind of teletype terminal).

*Source: A Brief History of Small Basic*

Terminals allowed direct interaction with a mainframe computer. Computer output was on paper and programs could be saved on a punched paper tape.

The original 1964 *BASIC* contained just 14 instructions  with one instruction per line, and variable names of one character based on the existing *FORTRAN* (1957) and *ALGOL* (1959) programming languages for  mainframe computers for  mathematical/scientific and business uses, but simplified for use by less mathematical or technically inclined users. FORTRAN was restricted to IF, DO and GOTO statements only, but had logical variables (TRUE or FALSE).

FORTRAN used English words as key words (like LIST, SAVE, RUN, END and PRINT) in the *syntax* of its instructions, and lines of program were numbered and executed in numerical sequence. Designed at first for mathematical programs, character strings were additionally incorporated from 1965. COBOL had only numbers and strings as data types, but its English-like lexicon and syntax made it easy to learn for business users.

The authors of the original *BASIC* did not copyright their work but instead actively promoted the language by making it free to industry, schools and others who could develop its functionality. Eventually, 'home' *BASIC* had been developed into a form containing all the functions described in the next chapter. Originally designed to be *compiled-*programs being converted into machine code and then executed as a whole- an important development was to implement the language as an *interpreter* with programs being executed line by line. This, together with an editor which made errors easy to spot and correct made *BASIC* more interactive and debugging easier. Widespread dissemination of the simple to use programming language quickly led to its popularization on the new minicomputers.

But this also resulted in many disparate forms of the original *BASIC* and so in 1974 ANSI (American National Standards Institute) issued specifications for a standardized, 'minimal' *BASIC* comprising the features common to the various versions to make programs 'portable' between different computers.

*BASIC* really took off with the advent of microcomputers from the mid-1970's. The 1975 version, known as *Altair BASIC*, was sold on cassette tape, produced by the to-become-famous Bill Gates of the now Microsoft Corporation and Paul Allen. This was the first to be used on the MITS *Altair 8800* microcomputer, based on the *Intel* 8080 8-bit microprocessor, initially with just 4kb of user memory available (compare this with the Gb of memory available on modern PCs, literally a million times more), shown below:

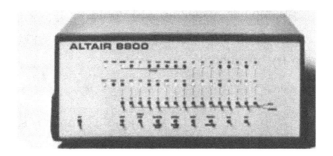

Altair 8800. Note the presence of switches and lights instead of keyboard!

[top] *Source:* http://en.wikipedia.org/wiki (accessed 3/1/2014)

[bottom] *Source: A Brief History of Small Basic*

Their compiled *BASIC* left enough memory for running both the program and storing the data. Gates and Allen set to work to produce *BASIC* versions that ran on other computers. By 1980, popular machines running versions of *BASIC* included the *Sinclair ZX80* (1980), *Commodore PET* (1977), *Apple* (1978), *Atari 400/800* (1978) and the *BBC* micro (1983). Applications for Micro-soft BASIC were published serially in computer magazine and could be typed into their computers by enthusiastic beginner programmers to try out at home.

Companies such as Apple Computer started to introduce *BASIC* on a ROM chip, so that the computer would on starting up display a *BASIC* command line. Others, such as the *Research Machines 380Z* loaded *BASIC* on disc into computer memory once the computer had booted up. *Micro-soft* (later to become *Microsoft* ), made its version of *BASIC* available on disc:

MSX BASIC version 3.0

*Source: http://en.wikipedia.org/*

The *Amstrad* PCW8256 used a 3" floppy disc to load *BASIC* into computer memory. Screen shots of the display before after BASIC has been loaded into computer memory are shown below:

Amstrad PCW8256 Monitor Display with CP/M prompt
*Source:* http://www.vintagecomputer.net/analog-digital.cfm  (accessed 3/1/2014)

```
CP/M Plus Amstrad Consumer Electronics plc
A>Basic

Mallard-80 BASIC with Jetsam Version 1.29
Copyright 1984 Locomotive Software Ltd

ok
```

Amstrad PCW8256 Monitor Display with BASIC loaded into memory from disc

But by the 1980s, most home ('micro'-) computers had a ROM *BASIC* interpreter, allowing the machines to boot directly into a *BASIC* user interface (compare this with GUI Graphics User Interface of modern home computers ('PC's)).

As user memory increased from 4 to 8 then 16kb and more, and greater processing power became available, more data bits could be manipulated and stored. The *Amstrad PCW* 8256, for example, could cope with numbers up to $\pm$ $10^{38}$ in mathematical operations. At its height, the popularity and ubiquity of *BASIC* can be appreciated from the one million-plus sales of the book *BASIC Computer Games* which could be copied into and executed on virtually any popular computer and run.

Although *BASIC* went on to be developed into more advanced forms such as Visual BASIC for use on modern GUI computers, the primary interest in this series of books on Historical Computing is confined to the early 'first generation' *BASIC* versions in common use during the era of microcomputers, and so these further developments will not be considered here.

## 2. STRUCTURE OF *BASIC*

The main syntax and features of a minimum version of *BASIC* will be described with illustrative simple examples. (The reader is welcome to copy the programs and run them on old computers or their PCs with little modification being required in most cases). These were found sufficient to write the more practical programs which are described in the next chapter. They are also sufficient to write more complex programs such as those described in later volumes of this series. Though the author used the *Amstrad* PCW8256, which happened to be given to her, as the 'old' computer in developing the programs, any of the machines popular at the time could have been used and can be used to run the *BASIC* programs printed out in full in the Appendices, with minimal, if any, modification.

The structure of *BASIC* with its English key words and numbered statements executed in numerical sequence make the language easy to learn for beginners. Simple programs to display a line of text such as:

10 PRINT "THIS IS MY FIRST PROGRAM IN BASIC"

can be written and successfully executed by typing RUN from the very outset. Lines can be numbered from 1-9999.

From this starting point, the main programming features of *BASIC* can be progressively introduced into the home computer beginner owner's programs. Characters can be held in a string variable represented by a letter and a dollar symbol:

20 A$="THIS IS MY FIRST PROGRAM IN BASIC"

30 PRINT A$

Numerical variables can be represented similarly, but without the dollar symbol. In fact more than one letter or letter-numeral combination (e.g. A1) can be used for a variable, but only the first two characters are significant. This still gives at least 286 distinct variables- very ample for most programming needs.

Numbers or strings can be fetched from the keyboard with the INPUT instruction:

10 INPUT A

20 PRINT A

*BASIC* has built in mathematical functions for arithmetic (+, -, / and * for multiplication), log base e (LOG) , trig functions (COS, SIN, TAN, and ATN for the inverse), absolute value (ABS) and integer value (INT):

10 INPUT A

20 INPUT B

30 ?C=A+B

The program above prompts the user to enter numerical values for A and B, adds them and stores the result in C before printing out the result. Note the use of ? as a shorter version of PRINT.

The value stored in a variable can be raised to a power, which can be positive, negative or fractional (for roots), by typing ^ after the variable name, followed by the power to which it is to be raised. So if A=81, ?A^.5 displays 9.

If an expression is repeatedly used in a program, it may be defined using DEF FN (meaning define function). For example, FN(X)=3*x^3+2*x^2+x+1 calculates the value of $3x^3+2x^2+x+1$ and stores the result in FN(X), which can be used just like any other variable, instead of the full expression $3x^3+2x^2+x+1$. For example ?FN(3) prints out 49 $(3^3+2.3^2+3+1)$.

*BASIC* can cope with numbers up about ±1E38, with a precision of at least 7 digits for positive numbers and 6 for negative numbers.

To help the programmer keep track of the rationale of the program, comments can be added using REM with their own line numbers which are ignored during execution:

```
10 REM PROGRAM TO ADD TWO NUMBERS
20 INPUT A
30 INPUT B
40 ?C=A+B
```

Often the programmer finds that s/he needs to insert a line between existing lines of the program. For example, it might be desired to extend the above program to include a third number stored in the variable X requiring an additional line before line 40. This line could be numbered 35, but then the neat equal numerical spacing (of 10 which is conventional) is lost. And of course, no more than eight new statements can be interposed between line numbers separated by 10. However the instruction RENUM allows the line numbers to be readjusted to the same sequence, with all references to line numbers within line statements being changed accordingly so as not to interfere with the operation of the program. For example RENUM (10,10) renumbers the lines of the program with intervals of 10, starting at line 10.

Numbers can be converted to strings using STR$, and vice versa using VAL. So

10 X=3.142

20 X$=STR$(X)

stores 3.142 in X$ as "3.142"

and adding the line

30 A=VAL(X$)

converts the string "3.142" in X$ to the number 3.142 which is stored in variable A. I found this facility very useful when programming the long division algorithm to cope with numbers of precision greater than that available on scientific calculators, as described in Chapter 4.

LEN returns the number of characters in the string, and MID$ can be used to return a part of the string.

In the above example, MID$(A$,2,3) returns ".142"- the first argument setting the beginning of the part of the string and second the number of characters to be returned. The arguments (2,3) can also be mathematical expressions.

*BASIC* like other computer languages excels in performing repetitive tasks efficiently, and contains the instruction GOSUB which can be used to access a block of statements called a *subroutine* from within the program over and over again, without the need to re-write the corresponding code each time it is used. For example,

```
10 REM ADD 2 SETS OF 2 NUMBERS

20 A=65

30 B=37

40 GOSUB 1000

50 A=34

60 B=67

70 GOSUB 1000

80 STOP
```

1000 ?A+B

1010 RETURN

Note the use of RETURN which returns control to the main program. Also STOP is used to terminate the program before it runs into line 1000.

A related instruction is GOTO which causes execution of the program to continue at the line number appended to GOTO.


Another important efficiency feature is *looping* which refers to a block of statements starting with FOR and ending with NEXT which executes the instructions in the lines between a number times given by the number appended to FOR. For example:

10 FOR I= 1 TO 10

20 ?"*"

30 NEXT I

displays ten stars. The arguments 1 and 10 in the FOR instruction can also be variables or mathematical expressions, and instead of counting up 1 by 1, the arguments of FOR may be appended with STEP to count in 2'2, 3's, etc., or count down instead of up.

For example:

```
10 REM LOOP COUNTS DOWN IN 2's,
DISPLAYING SINGLE ALTERNATE
CHARACTERS FROM A STRING IN
ORIGINAL AND THEN REVERSE ORDER

20 A$="PROGRAMS"

30 FOR I= 8 TO 2 STEP-2

40 ?MID$(A$,I,1)

50 NEXT I
```

However, this displays SAGR letter by letter down the screen and not across i8t as required, because at each execution of the PRINT statement, a 'carriage return' is executed. This can be prevented by adding a semi-colon at the end of the PRINT statement:

```
40 ?MID$(A$,I,1);
```

Note that it is important to include STEP followed by a numerical value if the second parameter of the IF statement is *greater* than the first, as the author found out the hard way. Depending on the version of *BASIC* this could otherwise cause the loop to count down anyway or just do nothing.

Loops can also be *nested*, that is to say there can be several loops within loops, with the inner most loop executed first. For example:

10 REM LOOP COUNTS DOWN IN 2's, DISPLAYING SINGLE ALTERNATE CHARACTERS FROM A STRING IN ORIGINAL AND THEN IN REVERSE ORDER

20 A$="PROGRAMS"

30 FOR I= 8 TO 2 STEP-2

35 FOR J=2 TO 8 STEP 2

40 ?MID$(A$,J,1);

45 NEXT J

47 ?MID$(A$,I,1);

50 NEXT I

*Arrays* may also be declared, in which each character behaves as though it has its own variable.

Arrays must be dimensioned with the DIM instruction before using them in the program. For example DIM A$(10) allocates space for 10 string variables A$(1) to A$(10). For example, such an array is used in the program illustrating DATA and READ statements described shortly.

Instead of continuing from the next line in the sequence, execution can continue at some other line chosen by the user if the test of some logical or mathematical condition is true, using the IF instruction. For example:

10 REM DO THREE LINES MAKE A RIGHT-ANGLED TRIANGLE?

20 INPUT A

30 INPUT B

40 INPUT C

50 REM USE PYTHAGORAS:

60 IF A*A+B*B=C*C THEN GOTO 100

70 ?"NOT A RIGHT-ANGLED TRIANGLE"

80 GOTO 20

100 ?"MAKE A RIGHT-ANGLED TRIANGLE"

The meanings of variables can be made clear by adding PRINT statements. For example,

10 ?"ENTER THE LENGTH OF THE FIRST LINE"

15 INPUT A

The program can be made much more compact and less time consuming to type in by concatenating two or more statements separated by colons instead of giving them their own line numbers, although its complexity is increased. So the two statements above might be combined in the single line

10 ?"ENTER THE LENGTH OF THE FIRST LINE":INPUT A

DATA together with READ instructions can be used to store data which can be retrieved from within the program. For example:

10 DIM A(11)

20 DATA 0,-1,2,3.9,-6.67,2.764,-20,7,2.22,-19

25 FOR I=1 TO 10

30 READ A(I)

35 NEXT I

40 ?A(4)

stores 10 numbers in the array variable A and then displays the the 4th (3.9). Note that A has been dimensioned for 11 characters, not 10. This is to avoid an error- which would stop the program from working correctly- due to the loop variable I being incremented to 11 at the end of the loop before testing this value against the 2nd argument in the

FOR statement, which, since it is greater than 10, causes execution of the statements within the loop to terminate.

Finally, the TAB instruction may be used to display character(s) at a chosen point on the screen. For example

10 ?TAB(20);

20 ?"*"

displays a star 20 character spaces from the left margin of the text area of the screen, or from the last printed position. Notice that TAB is used with a PRINT instruction. The argument may also be a mathematical expression such as ?TAB(2*A). As again the author found out the hard way when a messy output was obtained, the reader should note that some versions of *BASIC* will continue to print to the end of the line on encountering a new TAB instruction, others may resume printing on  a new line.

A most useful aspect of *BASIC* is that, since it is compiled and executed line by line, logical *sections* and even single lines of a program can be debugged without having to run the entire program, which would be the case in compiled languages- and if a bug existed anywhere in the program it would very likely not run. This in turn would force the programmer to review the instructions of the entire program, instead of focussing on a single, and therefore much more manageable aspect of its operation. The enabling *BASIC* facility is referred to as *Immediate Execution* mode, as opposed to *Deferred Execution* mode which refers to normal execution of a program consisting of numbered lines of instructions. For example, a program might contain a line of complex arithmetical statements which are very easy to get wrong, causing the program, if it runs at all, to run with a 'bug'. After typing in (without line numbers) appropriate values for the variables involved, the line can be typed in direct and can be immediately executed by typing [ENTER]. This makes it a simple matter to make changes to the line and see the result immediately, making for much less time consuming and much more efficient programming. As described in Volume III of this series, using the Immediate Execution mode of *BASIC* to debug programs performing fairly complicated mathematical operations which would operate as intended, made it much easier to program the same operations in a compiled language environment by transferring the logic used from the simpler programming *BASIC* environment to the more complex one .

## 3. RUNNING *BASIC* ON MODERN PCs

For those who don't have an old computer like the *Amstrad PCW8256*, the *Research Machines* 380Z or the *Apple II* (both shown below),

Apple II Microcomputer (1982)

*Source*: http://oldcomputers.net/appleii.html

(accessed 3/1/2014)

Research Machines 380Z Microcomputer (1981)

Source:
http://www.flickr.com/photos/andyretrocomputers/4691
892072/

(accessed 30/5/2013)

or one of the many other makes which used *BASIC* to enable users to write their own programs, a program which will install *BASIC* on a modern Windows [or Mac], *Vintbas* (short for vintage *BASIC*) (Kopnicky (2011)), is downloadable free from the www. The author also found the GUI Notepad editor much easier to use than *BASIC* command line editors and greatly facilitated the programming process. I used the *Vintbas* program to write new programs or re-write programs originally created on the *Amstrad PCW8256* micro-computer-word processor described in this book. *Vintbas* comes complete with instructions about how to install the software and debugging programs. Originally accessed in December, 2011, I found the instructions accompanying the download have easier ways of doing things, some of the more important of which are described below.

The *BASIC* program is typed into Notepad as statements, each with a line number, pressing [Enter] after each line. This must be saved as a **.bas** file **not** a .txt file by choosing 'All Files' and appending .bas to the chosen filename.

The program is executed from the Command Prompt, but first this needs to be set to the required filepath. All my *BASIC* programs for example are in C:\Users\pejt4\Basic_programs. Clicking on the Command Prompt, I found the filepath set to c:\. To alter it to that above, I right clicked on its icon, then Properties, and changed the filepath in the Start in: box to  C:\Users\pejt4\Basic_programs. Then in order to be able to quickly access the Command Prompt from the folder containing my *BASIC* programs, I right-clicked on the Command Prompt icon and 'copy'. Then in the Basic_programs folder 'paste' which installs a shortcut to the Command Prompt.

So, after clicking on the shortcut, the full filename of the *BASIC* program to be executed is typed in followed by [Enter]. Any bugs such as syntax errors and description together with their line numbers are displayed in the Command Prompt window to (indispensably) aid debugging. The Command Line debugger is shown below:

```
run_debug_basic_programs
Copyright (c) 2006 Microsoft Corporation.
All rights reserved.

c:\users\pejt4\Basic_programs>sfdp2.bas
!SYNTAX ERROR IN LINE 20, COLUMN 28
 UNEXPECTED END OF LINE

c:\users\pejt4\Basic_programs>
```

Readers intending to use the *Vintbas BASIC* programming environment to run programs should note that although this can be done by clicking on the icon of the .bas file and choosing to 'open with' vintbas, **this results in the premature closing of the program.** This can be avoided by an extra line in the Notepad .bas file containing an INPUT command causing a wait for a key to be pressed before the program closes, or by opening the file via the Command Prompt as already explained.

As mentioned earlier, I found the GUI *BASIC* programming environment much easier to use than the command line of the old computers for which *BASIC* was originally intended. For example, using the mouse to highlight, copy and paste, long statements in previous lines could be copied, pasted in, then changing just those aspects of the statement where the next line differed from the copied one, instead of having to re-type in the whole line. This made the initial writing of the program less tedious and less time consuming- particularly in the case of a long program. Furthermore, in debugging, lines numbers and contents could easily be changed by highlighting, cutting, copying and pasting.

I found that the different font styles and colours available made programming a more pleasant experience on the PC GUI desktop than the command line of micro-computers. Lines could highlighted to make them easier to locate amongst the many; longer and more realistic file names could be used than in command line *BASIC*- for example the *BASIC* used on the *Amstrad pcw 8256* allows a maximum of just 8 characters, so something like 'Fisher Exact Test' would have to be saved as, say, 'FISHEXAC'.

FIND on the EDIT menu in Notepad was useful for locating variables or expressions in a program, but could not be used to find a specific datum in DATA statements because, being separated by commas rather than spaces, they are not 'seen' as separate entities. But there is a big advantage in execution speed due to the speed of modern processors compared with the early ones. The difference is really noticeable when many data and/or long, complex mathematical processing is required, which could even make the same program running on a micro-computer impossibly slow to use (two statistical programs are described in the Volume II where this is the case).

A disadvantage of the *Vintbas* GUI *BASIC* programming environment used is that there is no immediate execution mode, which meant that programs could not easily be debugged section by section. For example, a subroutine could not be executed by itself in order to sort out the bugs in it without requiring the complete program to be executable in order to see the results of changes to the subroutine. Another result is that it is more of a nuisance to tidy up the numbering of program lines after inserting new lines between existing lines or deleting lines, since there is no RENUMBER instruction. Of course, neither de-bugging environment will pick up logical errors which do not cause the program not to run but result in an incorrect or unintended output. But having the deferred mode facility enables the programmer to check the values assigned to variables during its execution program after it finishes, since variables are only cleared when the program is RUN. This is helpful in narrowing down where bugs of this sort occur in the program. Though not important in the programs described in this series, in other programs the facility to RUN another program from within the program may be important, but the RUN instruction does not feature in *Vintbas*.

## 4. EXAMPLE *BASIC* PROGRAMS

These have been grouped together under the headings 'Mechanics', 'Finance', 'Number' and 'Geometry'. To illustrate *BASIC* programming on both the original computers on which it was used and its use on modern PCs, some of the programs were written on the *AMSTRAD PCW8256*, shown below-

Amstrad pcw8256 computer *Source: http://es.wikipedia.org/wiki/Amstrad_PCW_8256*

-Locomotive Software Ltd's Mallard-80 BASIC Version 1.29, 1984, and others in Notepad on a modern Windows PC running *Vintbas* vintage *BASIC* as explained earlier. The screen shots to be shown differ accordingly.

The two versions of *BASIC* are so similar that I was able to simply copy the code of a program running successfully on the *AMSTRAD* to Notepad for running under *Vintbas.*(In most cases, this was also true of the statistical programs in Volume II, though there were important exceptions).

The following programs is are intended to exemplify the use *BASIC* in programming and the variety of uses to which *BASIC* programs can be put. The programs are grouped under headings according to the type of task the program carries out, beginning with mechanics.

**Mechanics**

Everyday experience shows that when a load is suddenly applied the effect on whatever supports it is greater than if it is gradually applied. The effect is greater still if the load is released from a height above the support. The three situations are represented diagrammatically below:

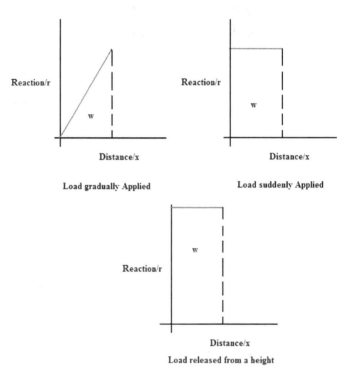

**Fig 1:** Graphs representing 3 modes of applying a load to a supporting surface

If the distance moved by the support due to reaction from the application of the load is x, the work done in the first case is represented by the area under the graph in the top left-hand figure, which is w.x/2. The effect on the support is therefore 1/2 that due to a load which is suddenly

applied, producing an amount of work equal w.x-
the situation in the above figure (top right). The
physical situation is shown diagrammatically
below:

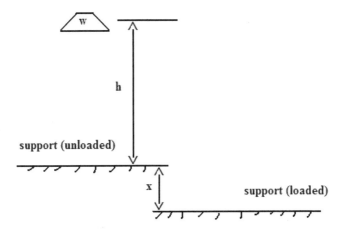

**Fig 2:** The Physical disposition of the weight and
support

If the load is released from a height h onto the
support, the potential energy due to the height of
the load above the support is added to the work
done on the support by the stationary (suddenly
applied) load.

This potential energy is w.h. So now we have a
reaction r on the support from the action of the load
which is given by:

$r.x/2 = w.(h+x)$.

44

Now the elasticity of the support k is given by r/x, hence x=r/k. Substituting this expression for x in the above equation gives:

$$r.r/2.k = w.(h+r/k),$$

from which $r^2 = 2k.w.h + 2w.r$ and so

$$r = \sqrt{2.k.w.h^2} + w$$

This is used in the program on p. 68 to calculate the reaction on a car boot floor (the support) when a weight is dropped onto it. A screen shot of the output is shown below:

```
ok
run "dumpload"
THE LOADING ON A CAR'S SUSPENSION WHEN  A WEIGHT IS DROPPED FROM A HEIGHT INTO THE BOC
ENTER THE WEIGHT DROPPED IN LBS? 70
ENTER THE HEIGHT  IN FT ABOVE THE BOOT FLOOR FROM WHICH THE WEIGHT IS DROPPED
? 3
ENTER THE CAR'S SUSPENSION'S ELASTICITY IN LBS/IN? 175
THE LOADING ON THE CAR BOOT IS 350  LBS
ok
```

## Finance

Borrowing money to purchase a house or paying for a purchase made by credit card can be costly, as one knows from experience. The underlying reason for this is, of course, that interest is compounded from year to year (or month to month) during the term of the loan.

Interest payments on credit card loans are calculated on a monthly basis and usually the loan company will quote a monthly interest rate together with an "A.P.R. equivalent" percentage rate. For example, the loan company might quote a monthly interest of 1.8% and an equivalent A.P.R. of 24%. The relationship between the two is as follows:

$$\left[\left(1 + \frac{\text{monthly interest rate (\%)}}{100}\right)^{12} - 1\right] \times 100 = \text{A.P.R.}$$

But just how much does a given amount borrowed cost in interest as a fraction (or multiple) of the amount borrowed when it has been paid off?

The monthly repayment on the loan is given by:

46

$$\frac{R.S.(1 + R)^n}{12[(1 + R)^n - 1}$$

where R is the annual rate of interest, S is the sum borrowed, and n is the duration (term) of the loan.

Interested readers might like to see how this formula is derived in the Appendix, p. 67.

This formula is used in the program on p. 69 which calculates the monthly repayments on a mortgage or credit card loan according to the option chosen by the user, given an annual rate of interest (Annual Percentage Rate A.P.R.) or monthly rate of interest supplied by the user. A screen shot of the program's output is shown below:

```
ok
run "credmort"
MORTGAGE/CREDIT CARD REPAYMENTS
IF MORTAGE ENTER [1]; IF CREDIT LOAN PRESS [2]? 2
TO USE AN ANNUAL PERCENTAGE RATE (A.P.R.) ENTER [1]; TO USE A MONTHLY INTEREST RATE
ENTER [2]? 2

ENTER THE MONTHLY INTEREST RATE IN  %? 1.8
ENTER THE SUM BORROWED IN POUNDS? 100
ENTER THE TERM OF THE LOAN IN YEARS? 3
MONTHLY REPAYMENTS ARE OF  4.2  POUNDS
TOTAL INTERST PAID IS  151.2  POUNDS
AFTER 3 YEARS YOU PAY 1.512  X THE AMOUNT BORROWED
ok
```

**Number 1.**

My calculator can be set to display input and output to a given number of *decimal* places (d.p.), but in order set the number of significant figures (s.f.) in displaying the result of a calculation, scientific notation must be used, changing the format of numbers keyed in, whereas an output in the same format as input may be desired. For example,

3.7621 x 4.3257 is output in normal display mode as 16.27371597. Switching to scientific mode and setting the number of d.p. results in the display:

$$1.63 \text{ x } 10^{01}$$

This gives a result correct to the desired 3 significant figures but the result required is 16.3.

The program on p. 70 displays a number input by the user to a given number of s.f. or d.p. as required. A screen shot of the output of the program is shown below:

```
run_debug_basic_programs
Program written by Dr.P.Trigger 8/1/2013
S.F. [1] OR D.P. [2]
? 1
ENTER NUMBER WITH NO LEADING OR TRAILING ZEROS? 16.27371597

TO HOW MANY FIGURES? 3
16.3 (TO  3 S.F. )


Press ENTER key to close
?
```

**Number 2.**

My 10-digit scientific calculator* has this limitation to the accuracy with which it can perform and display the result of calculations. For example suppose I want to know the result of dividing 12345678910 by 3.

The dividend is 11 digits long, and so the calculator will round up the result to 10 digits. In this case, the result displayed is 4115226303, giving the incorrect impression that 12345678910 is (exactly) divisible by 3. In fact, the true result is 4115226303 r 1, where 'r' stands for 'remainder' (or 4115226303 $^1/_3$ if you like).

Similarly, on the *Amstrad PCW 8256* when I type in x= 12345678910 and then ?x, the computer displays the number 1.2345678E10, and x/3 as 4.115226E10, rounding from 11 to 7 digits accuracy.

Supposing I need greater accuracy? *BASIC* enables data to be stored as strings which can be much more than 10 characters long. First the string has to be dimensioned so as to be allocated enough memory space to contain all the characters.

* a CASIO *fx-83 MS*

Let's be generous and type dim a$(50). If I now type in a$="12345678910" and then ?a$, the computer returns *all* 11 digits, as it will if a number up to 50 digits long is typed in.

But a string cannot be divided by 3, and as soon as the string is converted back into ordinary number, the problem of limited accuracy re-emerges.

One solution to this problem, as the filename of the following program suggests, is to use the familiar 'long division' algorithm which is used to perform division operations by hand. This is shown below for our example of 12345678910 ÷ 3:

51

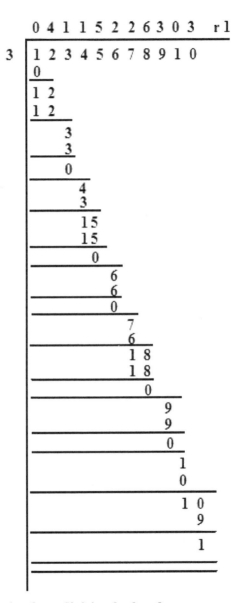

**Fig 3: Performing long division by hand**

This method is extremely tedious for dividends with many digits; I would not like to try it on, say,

1234567891011121314151617181920212324
(except to verify the correct operation of the program!).

But notice that only one digit (in this case) of the dividend is operated on at a time, not all 11. More digits will have to be 'brought down' from the dividend for divisors with more digits, but as long as there are not too many ( 7 or less -the focus of interest here is on very large *dividends*), the operations performed stay within the accuracy of the computer.

Thus, in the file longdiv, a print-out of which is on p. 72, only the digits to be brought down at each step of performing the above algorithm are retrieved from the string by converting the characters representing those digits numerically into actual numerical digits using the *BASIC* expression VAL(name of string variable) (see line 100 in the program print out). The quotient result of each step is then converted back into a string character and stored in a string variable which will at the finish contain the final result- and as we have seen this can be a very long series of digits. A screen shot of the output is shown below:

```
ok
run "longdiv.bas"
ENTER THE DIVIDEND? 13987342178509231456
ENTER THE DIVISOR? 37
13987342178509231456/37=00378036275094844093R 15
ok
```

## Number 3.

A decimal can be written down symbolically in an
exact form if it is a recurring decimal and the
recurring digits can be identified. For example,
instead of writing $^1/_{11}$ as 0.091 to 3 significant
figures, it can be written down exactly as symbol

$$0.\overline{909}$$

My calculator displays 0.09090909 when I key in

1 ÷ 11 and so in this case which digits are
recurring is fairly clear. But where there is a long
series of recurring digits, these may be difficult to
determine. For example,my calculator displays

0.142857142 in response to $^1/_7$, suggesting that the
digits 142 may be repeated, but because the
calculator runs out of accuracy it cannot be
determined from this whether any of 8, 5 or 7 are
also repeated. In fact, the recurring digits are
142857. Some decimal numbers have even longer
series of recurring digits, such as that representing,
say, $^2/_{23}$ , which has 22.

The program on p. 73 uses the long division
algorithm to compare the remainders of each step
with previous ones, because if two are the same,

the digits going into the quotient will recur. This is illustrated below in the case of the decimal number representing $^1/_7$:

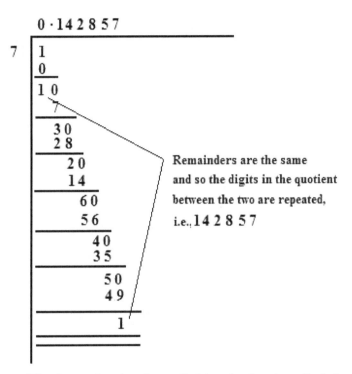

**Fig 4:** Performing long division by hand to find the recurring digits of a decimal number

A Screen Shot of the Program's Output is shown below:

56

# A Screen Shot of the Output of a Program to find the digits recurring in a decimal number:

```
ok
run "tesrecur.bas"
ENTER THE NUMERATOR
? 3
ENTER THE DENOMINATOR
? 7
 3 / 7 =0. 4  2  8  5  7  1  4  2  8  5  7  1  4  2  8  5  7  1  4  2  8  5  7 >>>

CHECKING FOR RECURRING DIGITS IN THE FIRST 100...

THE RECURRING DIGITS ARE:
 4   2   8   5   7   1
ok
```

## Number 4.

The program on p. 74 generates a series of prime numbers whose length is determined by the user, up to a thousand primes. Beginning with 2, it does this by testing each consecutive whole number (3,4,5,...,) for divisibility by a (smaller) prime number. But it is only necessary to use divisors up to the square root of the dividend (i.e. of the number tested) in value. For example, 25 need only tested for divisibility by 2, 3 and 5. A screen shot of the output is shown below:

```
run_debug_basic_programs
Microsoft Windows [Version 6.0.6001]
Copyright (c) 2006 Microsoft Corporation.  All rights reserved.

c:\users\pejt4\Basic_programs>genprime.bas
HOW MANY PRIMES? (MAX. 1,000)
? 25
  2  3  5  7  11  13  17  19  23  29  31  37  41  43  47  53  59
 61  67  71  73  79  83  89  97

c:\users\pejt4\Basic_programs>
```

**Number 5.**

The old Roman number system is still quite commonplace, not only in historical manuscripts or on artefacts, but for example in dating TV programs and cinematic films, and in the pagination of books. It is useful to know what these numbers are in the more familiar denary number system, and vice versa.

The conversion from Roman to denary number is basically a translation of each Roman symbol (I, V, X, L, C, D and M) into its the denary value and summation of the result. But provision must be made to subtract the value of a lower order symbol where this is placed immediately to the left of the following symbol. For example, XC is not 10+100 but -10+100. In addition, in the program to convert denary to Roman number there is a rule of combination of pairs of symbols used in this way which must be taken account of. This rule is that symbols *one* order of magnitude in value or lower may precede a given symbol if the value of the pair of symbols cannot be represented by a single lower order symbol (e.g. VX is just V) or a combination of lower order symbols containing three or fewer repeated symbols (e.g. denary 4 is not (in common usage) IIII but IV, 40 is not XXXX but XL), otherwise a symbol can be preceded only by a symbol *two* orders of magnitude lower. Examples of allowable combinations are CD (denary 400) (where C is one order of magnitude less than D) and IX (denary 9) (where I is *two* orders of magnitude lower than X, because V, though one order of magnitude less than V, VX is simply V as mentioned above). Examples of disallowed combinations are XM intended to represent denary 1990 which according to the rule above is represented by MCMXC, and LD intended to represent denary 450 which is correctly represented by CDL.

Screen shots of the output of a program to convert Roman number to denary and denary number to Roman on pp. 75-6 are shown below:

60

A screen shot of the program converting Roman to denary number

```
ok
run "romden.bas"
CONVERTS ROMAN TO DENARY NUMBER
AFTER EACH ROMAN NUMERAL PRESS [RETURN]
AFTER THE LAST ROMAN NUMERAL PRESS [RETURN] TWICE
? M
M? C
MC? M
MCM? L
MCML? X
MCMLX? X
MCMLXX? X
MCMLXXX? V
MCMLXXXV? I
MCMLXXXVI? I
MCMLXXXVII? I
MCMLXXXVIII?
MCMLXXXVIIICALCULATING...
MCMLXXXVIII 1988
ok
```

A screen shot of the program converting denary number to Roman number:

```
ok
run "denrom.bas"
DENARY TO ROMAN NUMBER
ENTER A NUMBER <9999? 1988
MCMLXXXVIII
ok
```

## Geometry 1.

Vectors may be represented in Cartesian (a + ib) or polar form (r<θ). Adding vectors in Cartesian form to find their resultant is very straight forward since it is only necessary to add the corresponding real parts and imaginary parts of the vectors added. For example, (3 + 2i) + (4 - 3i) = (3 + 4) + (4 - 3)i = 7 - i. Adding vectors in polar form is not so and their conversion from

r.(cos θ + sin θ) into Cartesian form is required before adding. The result may then be converted back into polar form. The process is complicated further by the need to ensure that θ corresponds to the correct quadrant and when one vector may be in Cartesian form and the other in polar form.

The program on p. 77 adds vectors in a mix of Cartesian and polar forms and outputs the result in both forms, as exemplified in a screen shot of the program's output below:

62

## A Screen Shot of the Output of the program adding vectors in a mix of Cartesian and polar forms

```
ok
run "vecadd.bas"
TO SUBTRACT A VECTOR, MULTIPLY ITS COMPONENTS OR MAGNITUDE BY 1 BEFORE ENTERING


HOW MANY VECTORS TO BE ADDED?
? 2
IS VECTOR 1  IN CARTESIAN FORM [PRESS 1] OR POLAR (ANGLE) FORM [PRESS 2]?
? 1
ENTER THE i COMPONENT OF THE VECTOR 1
? 3
ENTER THE j COMPONENT OF THE VECTOR 1
? 4
IS VECTOR 2  IN CARTESIAN FORM [PRESS 1] OR POLAR (ANGLE) FORM [PRESS 2]?
? 2
ENTER THE MAGNITUDE OF THE VECTOR 2
? 2
ENTER THE ANGLE OF THE VECTOR 2
? 30
THE RESULTANT IN CARTESIAN FORM IS 4.732051 i 5 j
THE RESULTANT IN POLAR FORM IS 6.884207 < 46.577106 deg

ok
```

**Geometry 2.**

Another useful geometry program finds the angles and sides of any triangle, given at least two sides and one angle or 3 sides, using the cosine rule

$$c^2 = a^2 + b^2 + 2.a.b.\cos C,$$

where a, b and c denote the lengths of the sides and A, B and C the angle opposite the corresponding side as shown below:

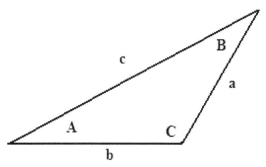

**Fig 5:** Symbols used for the angles and sides of a triangle

If any angle or side is unknown, the user enters 0 for that side or angle. The screen shot below shows the output of the program where C=120 deg, B=30 deg and C=10:

64

## A Screen Shot of the Output of the Program which finds the sides and angles of a triangle

```
ok
run "solvtri.bas"
ENTER SIDE A (IF UNKNOWN TYPE 0)? 0
ENTER SIDE B (IF UNKNOWN TYPE 0)? 0
ENTER SIDE C (IF UNKNOWN TYPE 0)? 10
ENTER ANGLE A IN DEGREES (IF UNKNOWN TYPE 0)? 0
ENTER ANGLE B IN DEGREES (IF UNKNOWN TYPE 0)? 30
ENTER ANGLE C IN DEGREES (IF UNKNOWN TYPE 0)? 120


A            B            C            A (DEG)      B (DEG       C (DEG)
---------------------------------------------------------------------------
5.774        5.774        10           30           30           120

(SIDES ARE TO 3 D.P., ANGLES ARE TO 1 D.P.)
ok
```

A print out of the program is shown on p. 78.

# 5. CONCLUSION

The original *BASIC* was developed to enable non-technical users to write programs- an activity which previously had been the preserve of those with appropriate scientific and mathematical expertise. As such *BASIC* was designed to incorporate features like English key words and numbered line statements which would not only make programs easy to write, but would be suited to the more interactive display-based time sharing system instead of the previous batch system with its punched cards and slow job turn-around.

Because the *BASIC* language was quick to learn easy to use, development of its functionality whilst maintaining portability between different makes of machines continued apace for home 'micro'computers, and at the height of its popularity it provided the principle user interface for millions world-wide.

This volume has shown how with a handful of simple instructions, a *BASIC* programming environment can be used to expedite the writing of successful computer programs which perform useful and even quite complicated tasks. In the 'useful' category come the miscellaneous examples described here, and the programming of non-parametric statistical tests in *BASIC* which are the subject of Volume II of this series. In the category of 'complicated tasks' come the programming of mathematical methods to invert matrices with complex elements, to solve higher order simultaneous equations and to solve higher order polynomial equations described in Volume III in, for example, tackling practical problems in Engineering Science.

# 6 a. APPENDIX 1: DERIVATIONS

## Derivation of a formula for the monthly repayments on a mortgage or credit card loan.

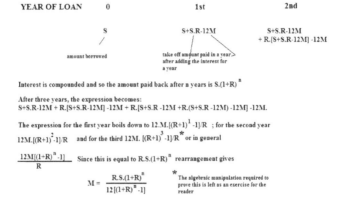

| YEAR OF LOAN | 0 | 1st | 2nd |
|---|---|---|---|
| | S | S+S.R-12M | S+S.R-12M + R.[S+S.R-12M] -12M |
| | amount borrowed | take off amount paid in a year after adding the interest for a year | |

Interest is compounded and so the amount paid back after n years is $S.(1+R)^n$

After three years, the expression becomes:
S+S.R-12M + R.[S+S.R-12M] -12M + R.[S+S.R -12M +R.(S+S.R -12M) -12M] -12M.

The expression for the first year boils down to $12.M.[(R+1)^1 -1]/R$ ; for the second year $12M.[(R+1)^2 -1]/R$ and for the third $12M. [(R+1)^3 -1]/R$ * or in general

$\frac{12M[(1+R)^n -1]}{R}$ Since this is equal to $R.S.(1+R)^n$ rearrangement gives

$$M = \frac{R.S.(1+R)^n}{12[(1+R)^n -1]}$$

\* The algebraic manipulation required to prove this is left as an exercise for the reader

68

# 6 b. APPENDIX 2: PRINT-OUTS

Program to calculate the loading on a car suspension when a weight in dropped into the boot

```
10 ?"THE LOADING ON A CAR'S SUSPENSION WHEN A WEIGHT IS DROPPED FROM A HEIGHT INTO THE BOOT"
20 GOSUB 220
30 REM
40 ?"ENTER THE WEIGHT DROPPED IN LBS";
50 INPUT W:Y=1:IF W<0 THEN 200
70 ?"ENTER THE HEIGHT IN FT ABOVE THE BOOT FLOOR FROM WHICH THE WEIGHT IS DROPPED"
80 INPUT H:Y=2:IF H<0 THEN 200
90 IF H>3 THEN 230
100 ?"ENTER THE CAR'S SUSPENSION'S ELASTICITY IN LBS/IN";
110 INPUT K:Y=3:IF K<0 THEN 200
120 R=SQR(W*W+2*K*W*H)+W
130 IF R>6*K THEN 160
140 ?"THE LOADING ON THE CAR BOOT IS";INT(R+.5);" LBS"
150 IF R<6*K THEN STOP
160 FOR J=1 TO 10:?"WARNING!";
170 GOSUB 260:?:GOSUB 260:IF J=10 THEN 250
180 NEXT J
190 GOTO 40
200 ?"IMPOSSIBLE!"
210 GOSUB 220
220 FOR I=1 TO 2500:NEXT I:RETURN
230 ?"TOO HIGH!":GOTO 70
240 GOSUB 220:GOTO 50
250 ?:?:? INT(R+.5);"LBS OVERLOADS THE BOOT":?:?:?:?:GOTO 40
260 FOR I=1 TO 20:NEXT I:RETURN
```

# Program to calculate mortgage/credit card repayments

```
10 ?"MORTGAGE/CREDIT CARD REPAYMENTS"
20 ?"IF MORTAGE ENTER [1]; IF CREDIT LOAN PRESS [2]";
30 INPUT ACCOUNT
40 IF ACOUNT=1 THEN 100
50 ?"TO USE AN ANNUAL PERCENTAGE RATE (A.P.R.) ENTER [1]; TO USE A MONTHLY
INTEREST RATE ENTER [2]";
70 IF RATE<>1 THEN 120
60 INPUT RATE
80 ?"ENTER A.P.R. IN %";
90 INPUT R:GOTO 140
100 ?"ENTER INTEREST RATE IN %"
110 INPUT R:GOTO 140
120 ?"ENTER THE MONTHLY INTEREST RATE IN  %";
130 INPUT R:R=100*((1+R/100)^12-1)
140 ?"ENTER THE SUM BORROWED IN POUNDS";
150 INPUT S
160 ?"ENTER THE TERM OF THE LOAN IN YEARS";
170 INPUT N
180 R=R/100
210 X=M:GOSUB 1000:M=X
200 M=S*R*(1+R)^N/(12*((1+R)^N-1))
220 ?"MONTHLY REPAYMENTS ARE OF ";M;" POUNDS"
230 ?"TOTAL INTERST PAID IS ";M*12*N;" POUNDS"
240 X=12*M*N:GOSUB 1000
250 ?"AFTER";N;"YEARS YOU PAY";X/S;" X THE AMOUNT BORROWED"
300 STOP
1000 X=INT (X)+INT (100*(X-INT(X))+.5)/100:RETURN
```

# Program to round a number to a given number of significant figures

```
SFDP - Notepad
File  Edit  Format  View  Help
10 REM*** CALCULATES A VALUE TO A GIVEN NUMBER OF S.F. OR D.P. ***
15 ?"Program written by Dr.P.Trigger 8/1/2013"
20 ?"S.F. [1] OR D.P. [2]":INPUT A
30 ?"ENTER NUMBER WITH NO LEADING OR TRAILING ZEROS";
40 INPUTX$
50 ?:?"TO HOW MANY FIGURES";:INPUT M
60 M1=M
70 IF VAL(X$)>=1 THEN 160
80 IF VAL(X$)<1 THEN Z=VAL(X$)
90 IF A=1 THEN GOSUB 380:GOTO 110
100 I=2
110 M=M+I-2:GOSUB 310:M=M-I+2
120 IF Z=0 AND A<>1 THEN M=M+1
130 ?STR$(Z);:GOSUB 530:GOSUB 430
140 IF A<>1 THEN I=3
141 IF LEN(STR$(Z))-I+2>M THEN 700
150 FOR J=LEN(STR$(Z))-I+1 TO M:?"0";:NEXT J:GOSUB 590:GOTO 700
160 FOR I=1 TO LEN(X$)+1
170 IF MID$(X$,I,1)="." THEN D=I:GOTO 190
180 NEXT I
190 IF D=0 THEN Z=VAL(X$)/10^(LEN(X$)):GOSUB 310:?STR$(Z*10^M);:FOR I=M+1 TO
LEN(X$):?"0";:NEXT I:?" (TO ";M;"S.F. )":GOTO 700
200 IF A<>1 THEN M=M+D-1
210 Z=VAL(X$)/(10^(D-1))
220 GOSUB 310
221 z=z*10^(D-1)
240 ? MID$(STR$(Z),2,M+1);
245 IF LEN(STR$(Z))<=M THEN GOSUB 470
250 IF A<>1 AND INT(Z)=Z THEN M=M-D+1
260 IF A<>1 THEN M=M+D-1:GOSUB 530
270 IF A<>1 THEN GOSUB 590:GOTO 700
280 IF M>LEN(STR$(Z))-1 THEN ?".";
290 IF LEN(STR$(Z))<=M THEN FOR I=LEN(STR$(Z)) TO M:?"0";:NEXT I
300 ?" (TO ";M;"S.F. )":GOTO 700
310 Y=INT(Z)
320 Z=Z-INT(Z)
330 Z=Z*10^M
340 Z=INT(Z+0.500004)
350 Z=Z/10^M
360 Z=Z+Y
370 RETURN
380 FOR I=2 TO LEN(X$)
390 IF MID$(X$,I,1)<>"0" THEN 420
400 NEXT I
420 RETURN
430 FOR I=4 TO LEN(STR$(Z))
440 IF MID$(STR$(Z),I,1)<>"0" THEN 460
450 NEXT I:RETURN
460 I=I-1:RETURN
470 X=LEN(STR$(Z))-1:
480 FOR I=1 TO LEN(STR$(Z))
490 IF MID$(STR$(Z),I,1)="." THEN X=X-1:GOTO 510
500 NEXT I:RETURN
```

```
510 FOR I=X+1 TO M:?"o";
520 NEXT I:RETURN
530 IF Z<>INT(Z) THEN 580
540 IF M<>LEN(STR$(Z))-1 THEN ?".";
550 IF A<>1 THEN M=M1+1
560 FOR J=1 TO M-1:?"o";:NEXT J:GOSUB 590:GOTO 700
570 GOTO 700
580 RETURN
590 IF A<>1 THEN ?" (TO";M1;"d.p.)":GOTO 610
600 ?" (TO";M1;"S.F.)"
610 RETURN
700 ?:?
710 ?"Press ENTER key to close":INPUTA$:
```

# Program to perform division on long numbers with a precision outside normal calculator range

```
10 REM DIVIDES ONE NUMBER BY ANOTHER TO GIVE A QUOTIENT AND REMAINDER
20 DIM QUOT$(500):DIM NUM$(500)
30 ?"ENTER THE DIVIDEND";
40 INPUT NUM$
50 FOR I=1 TO LEN(NUM$)
60 NUM$(I)=MID$(NUM$,I,1)
70 NEXT I
80 ?:?:?"ENTER THE DIVISOR";
90 INPUT DIV
100 X=VAL(NUM$(1))
110 FOR I=1 TO LEN(NUM$)
120 QUOT$(I)=STR$(INT(X/DIV))
130 X=X-VAL(QUOT$(I))*DIV
140 X=X*10+VAL(NUM$(I+1))
150 NEXT I
160 X=X/10
170 FOR J=1 TO I:?LEFT$(NUM$(J),1);:NEXT j:?"/";MID$(STR$(DIV),2,LEN(STR$(DIV)));"=";
180 FOR J=1 TO I:QUOT$=QUOT$+RIGHT$(QUOT$(J),1):NEXT j:?QUOT$;
190 ?"R";X
```

# Program to find the digits recurring in a decimal number

```
10 REM TESTS FOR A RECURRING DECIMAL GIVEN AN INPUT FRACTION
20 ?"ENTER THE NUMERATOR"
30 INPUT N
40 ?"ENTER THE DENOMINATOR"
50 INPUT D
60 IF N>=D THEN ?"A PROPER FRACTION IS REQUIRED":GOTO 20
70 N1=N:D1=D:DIM A(3)
80 IF D>50 THEN E=50:GOTO 100
90 E=D
100 DIM Q(2*E+10):DIM N(2*E+10)
110 M=2*E+10
120 ?N1;"/";D1;"=0.";
130 FOR I=1 TO M
140 Q=N/D
150 IF Q>=1 THEN Q(I)=INT(N/D):N=N-INT(N/D)*D:N(I)=N:GOTO 170
160 N(I)=N:Q(I)=0
170 IF N=INT(N/D)*D AND I<>0 THEN ?Q(I):STOP
180 IF I<>1 THEN ?Q(I);
190 N=N*10:NEXT I
200 ?">>>"
210 ?:?"CHECKING FOR RECURRING DIGITS IN THE FIRST 100..."
220 FOR I=2 TO M-1
230 FOR J=I+1 TO M
240 IF N(J)=N(I) THEN K=K+1:A(K)=J:IF K=2 THEN 280
250 NEXT J
260 NEXT I
270 ?"NO RECURRING DIGITS FOUND":STOP
280 REM
290 ?:?:?"THE RECURRING DIGITS ARE:"
300 FOR I=A(1) TO A(2)-1

310 ?Q(I);
320 NEXT I
330 STOP
340 ?N1;"/";D1;"=0.";
350 FOR I=2 TO M
360 ?Q(I);
370 NEXT I
380 RETURN
```

# Program generating a sequence of the first n prime numbers, where n is user-determined

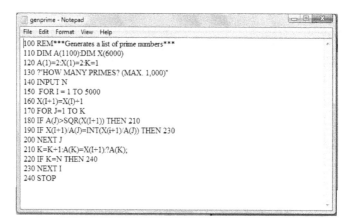

```
genprime - Notepad
File   Edit   Format   View   Help
100 REM***Generates a list of prime numbers***
110 DIM A(1100):DIM X(6000)
120 A(1)=2:X(1)=2:K=1
130 ?"HOW MANY PRIMES? (MAX. 1,000)"
140 INPUT N
150  FOR I = 1 TO 5000
160 X(I+1)=X(I)+1
170 FOR J=1 TO K
180 IF A(J)>SQR(X(I+1)) THEN 210
190 IF X(I+1)/A(J)=INT(X(i+1)/A(J)) THEN 230
200 NEXT J
210 K=K+1:A(K)=X(I+1):?A(K);
220 IF K=N THEN 240
230 NEXT I
240 STOP
```

## Program to convert Roman number to denary

```
10 ?"CONVERTS ROMAN TO DENARY NUMBER"
20 ?"AFTER EACH ROMAN NUMERAL PRESS [RETURN]"
30 ?"AFTER THE LAST ROMAN NUMERAL PRESS [RETURN] TWICE"
40 DIM A$(50)
50 FOR I=1 TO 50:INPUT A$(I)
60 FOR K=1 TO I:?A$(K);
70 NEXT K:IF A$(I)="" THEN 90
80 NEXT I
90 ?"CALCULATING...";
100 FOR K=1 TO I:IF A$(K)="M" THEN S=S+1000:GOSUB 220
110 IF A$(K)="D" THEN S=S+500:GOSUB 220
120 IF A$(K)="C" THEN S=S+100:GOSUB 240
130 IF A$(K)="L" THEN S=S+50:GOSUB 240
140 IF A$(K)="X" THEN S=S+10:GOSUB 260
150 IF A$(K)="V" THEN S=S+5:GOSUB 260
160 IF A$(K)="I" THEN S=S+1
170 NEXT K
180 ?
190 FOR K=1 TO I-1:?A$(K);
200 NEXT K:?S
210 STOP
220 IF A$(K-1)="C" THEN S=S-200
230 RETURN
240 IF A$(K-1)="X" THEN S=S-20
250 RETURN
260 IF A$(K-1)="I" THEN S=S-2
270 RETURN
```

## Program to convert denary number to Roman

```
10 ?"DENARY TO ROMAN NUMBER"
20 DIM A$(3,9)
30 DATA "C","CC","CCC","CD","D","DC","DCC","DCCC","CM"
40 DATA "X","XX","XXX","XL","L","LX","LXX","LXXX","XC"
50 DATA "I","II","III","IV","V","VI","VII","VIII","IX"
60 FOR I=1 TO 3:FOR J=1 TO 9:READ A$(I,J):NEXT J:NEXT I
70 ?:?"ENTER A NUMBER <9999";
80 INPUT Z:IF Z>9999 THEN 70
90 IF Z<=0 THEN 70
100 X=INT(Z/1000):IF X<1 THEN 130
110 FOR I=1 TO X:?"M";
120 NEXT I
170 D=INT(Z-X*1000-B*100-C*10):IF D<1 THEN 190
140 I=1:J=B:GOSUB 200
150 C=INT((Z-X*1000-B*100)/10):IF C<1 THEN 170
130 B=INT((Z-X*1000)/100):IF B<1 THEN 150
160 I=2:J=C:GOSUB 200
180 I=3:J=D:GOSUB 200
190 GOTO 220
200 ?A$(I,J);
210 RETURN
220 STOP
```

# Program to add vectors in a mix of Cartesian and polar forms

```
10 REM ADDS/SUBTRACTS MIXED VECTORS (CARTESIAN/POLAR)
20 PI=3.141592654
30 ?"TO SUBTRACT A VECTOR, MULTIPLY ITS COMPONENTS OR MAGNITUDE BY 1
BEFORE ENTERING":?:?
40 ?:?:?"HOW MANY VECTORS TO BE ADDED?"
50 INPUT N
60 DIM X(N):DIM Y(N)
70 FOR I= 1 TO N
80 ?"IS VECTOR";I;" IN CARTESIAN FORM [PRESS 1] OR POLAR (ANGLE) FORM [PRESS 2]?"
90 INPUT A
100 IF A=2 THEN GOSUB 1000:GOTO 150
110 ?"ENTER THE i COMPONENT OF THE VECTOR";I
120 INPUT X(I)
130 ?"ENTER THE j COMPONENT OF THE VECTOR";I
140 INPUT Y(I)
150 NEXT I
160 FOR I=1 TO N
170 XS=XS+X(I):YS=YS+Y(I)
180 NEXT I
200 R=SQR(XS*XS+YS*YS)
210 IF XS=0 AND YS>0 THEN TH=PI/2:GOTO 250
220 IF XS=0 AND YS<0 THEN TH=-PI/2:GOTO 250
230 IF XS=0 AND YS=0 THEN TH=0:GOTO 270
240 TH=ATN(YS/XS)
250 IF XS<0 THEN TH=TH+PI
260 IF TH>PI THEN TH=TH-2*PI
270 DEG=TH*180/PI
280 IF YS=0 AND XS<0 THEN DEG=180:TH=-TH
290 ?"THE RESULTANT IN CARTESIAN FORM IS";XS;"i";YS;"j"
300 ?"THE RESULTANT IN POLAR FORM IS";R;"<";DEG;"deg"

310 STOP
1000 ?"ENTER THE MAGNITUDE OF THE VECTOR";I
1010 INPUT R
1020 ?"ENTER THE ANGLE OF THE VECTOR";I
1030 INPUT TH
1040 X(I)=R*COS(TH*PI/180)
1050 Y(I)=R*SIN(TH*PI/180)
1060 RETURN
```

# Program to find the angles and sides of a triangle

```
10 DEF FN F(X)=INT(10*X+.5)/10
20 DEF FN G(X)=INT(1000*X+.5)/1000
30 REM FINDS REMAINING ANGLES AND SIDES OF A TRIANGLE
40 PI=3.141592
50 ?"ENTER SIDE A (IF UNKNOWN TYPE 0)";
60 INPUT AA
70 IF AA=0 THEN K=K+1
80 ?"ENTER SIDE B (IF UNKNOWN TYPE 0)";
90 INPUT BB
100 IF BB=0 THEN K=K+1
110 ?"ENTER SIDE C (IF UNKNOWN TYPE 0)";
120 INPUT CC
130 IF CC=0 THEN K=K+1
140 ?"ENTER ANGLE A IN DEGREES (IF UNKNOWN TYPE 0)";
150 INPUT A
160 IF A=0 THEN K1=K1+1
170 ?"ENTER ANGLE B IN DEGREES (IF UNKNOWN TYPE 0)";
180 INPUT B
190 IF B=0 THEN K1=K1+1
200 ?"ENTER ANGLE C IN DEGREES (IF UNKNOWN TYPE 0)";
210 INPUT C
220 IF C=0 THEN K1=K1+1
230 IF K=2 OR K=1 AND K1=1 THEN GOSUB 300:GOSUB 2050:STOP
240 IF K=1 THEN GOSUB 690:GOSUB 2050:STOP
250 IF K=0 THEN GOSUB 1290:GOSUB 2050:STOP
260 ?"AT MINIMUM, NEED ONE SIDE AND TWO ANGLES"
270 ?"OR TWO SIDES AND AN APPROPRIATE ANGLE"
280 ?"OR ALL THREE SIDES"
290 STOP
300 IF AA=0 THEN GOTO 430

310 IF B=0 OR C=0 THEN GOTO 350
320 A=180-(B+C)
330 GOSUB 1960
340 RETURN
350 IF A=0 OR C=0 THEN GOTO 390
360 B=180-(A+C)
370 GOSUB 1960
380 RETURN
390 IF A=0 OR B=0 THEN GOTO 1920
400 C=180-(B+A)
410 GOSUB 1960
420 RETURN
430 IF BB=0 THEN GOTO 570
440 IF B=0 OR C=0 THEN GOTO 480
450 A=180-(B+C)
```

```
450 A=180-(B+C)
460 GOSUB 1990
470 RETURN
480 IF A=0 OR C=0 THEN GOTO 520
490 B=180-(A+C)
500 GOSUB 1990
510 RETURN
520 C=180-(B+A)
530 IF A=0 OR B=0 THEN 1920
540 C=180-(B+A)
550 GOSUB 1990
560 RETURN
570 IF B=0 OR C=0 THEN GOTO 610
580 A=180-(B+C)
590 GOSUB 2020
600 RETURN
610 IF A=0 OR C=0 THEN GOTO 650
620 B=180-(C+A)
630 GOSUB 2020
640 RETURN
650 IF A=0 OR B=0 THEN 1920
660 C=180-(B+A)
670 GOSUB 2020
680 RETURN
690 IF AA=0 THEN 720
700 IF BB=0 THEN 820
710 IF CC=0 THEN 920
720 IF A=0 THEN 1020
730 AA=SQR(BB*BB+CC*CC-2*AA*CC*COS(A*PI/180))
740 B=SIN(A*PI/180)
750 B=BB*B/AA
760 B=B/SQR(1-B*B)
770 B=ATN(B)
780 IF SQR(AA*AA+CC*CC-2*AA*CC*COS(B))<(BB-.05) THEN b=PI-B
790 B=B*180/PI
800 C=180-(A+B)
810 RETURN
820 IF B=0 THEN 1440
830 BB=SQR(AA*AA+CC*CC-2*AA*CC*COS(B*PI/180))
840 C=SIN(B*PI/180)
850 C=CC*C/BB
860 C=C/SQR(1-C*C)
870 C=ATN(C)
880 IF SQR(AA*AA+BB*BB-2*AA*BB*COS(C))<(CC-.05) THEN C=PI-C
890 C=C*180/PI
900 A=180-(B+C)
910 RETURN
920 IF C=0 THEN 1680
930 CC=SQR(AA*AA+BB*BB-2*AA*BB*COS(C*PI/180))
940 A=SIN(C*PI/180)
950 A=AA*A/CC
```

```
960 A=A/SQR(1-A*A)
970 A=ATN(A)
980 IF SQR(AA*AA+CC*CC-2*CC*BB*COS(A))<(AA-.05) THEN A=PI-A
990 A=A*180/PI
1000 B=180-(A+C)
1010 RETURN
1020 IF C=0 THEN 1160
1030 IF (2*BB*COS(C*PI/180))^2<4*(BB*BB-CC*CC) THEN AA1=BB*COS(C*PI/180):GOTO
1070
1040 AA1=BB*COS(C*PI/180)+SQR((2*BB*COS(C*PI/180))^2-4*(BB*BB-CC*CC))/2
1050 AA1=BB*COS(C*PI/180)-SQR((2*BB*COS(C*PI/180))^2-4*(BB*BB-CC*CC))/2
1060 IF AA1 AND AA2>0 THEN 1940
1070 B=SIN(C*PI/180)
1080 B=BB*B/CC
1090 IF B>=1 THEN B=PI/2:GOTO 1120
1110 B=ATN(B)
1100 B=B/SQR(1-B*B)
1120 IF SQR(AA1*AA1+CC*CC-2*CC*AA1*COS(B))<BB-.05 THEN B=PI-B
1130 B=B*180/PI:AA=AA1
1140 A=180-(B+C)
1150 RETURN
1160 IF B=0 THEN ?"gIVEN 2 SIDES, MUST HAVE AT LEAST ONE ANGLE":STOP
1170 AA1=CC*COS(B*PI/180)+SQR((2*CC*COS(B*PI/180))^2-4*(CC*CC-BB*BB))/2
1180 AA2=CC*COS(B*PI/180)-SQR((2*CC*COS(B*PI/180))^2-4*(CC*CC-BB*BB))/2
1190 IF AA1 AND AA2>0 THEN 1940
1200 C=SIN(B*PI/180)
1210 C=CC*C/BB
1220 C=C/SQR(1-C*C)
1230 C=ATN(C)
1240 IF SQR(AA1*AA1+BB*BB-2*BB*AA1*COS(C))<(CC-.05) THEN C=PI-C
1250 C=C*180/PI
1260 A=180-(C+B)
1270 AA=AA1
1280 RETURN
1290 A=(BB*BB+CC*CC-AA*AA)/(2*BB*CC)
1300 IF A<0 THEN A=-A
1310 IF A>.9999999 THEN A=.9999999
1320 A=SQR(1-A*A)/A
1330 A=ATN(A)
1340 IF SQR(BB*BB+CC*CC-2*BB*CC*COS(A))<(AA-.05) THEN A=PI-A
1350 B=BB*SIN(A)/AA
1360 IF B>.9999999 THEN B=.9999999
1370 B=B/SQR(1-B*B)
1380 B=ATN(B)
1390 IF SQR(AA*AA+CC*CC-2*AA*CC*COS(B))<(BB-.05) THEN B=PI-B
1400 B=180*B/PI
1410 A=180*A/PI
1420 C=180-(A+B)
1430 RETURN
1440 IF A=0 THEN1560
1450 BB1=AA*COS(A*PI/180)+SQR((2*CC*COS(A*PI/180))^2-4*(CC*CC-AA*AA))/2
```

```
1460 BB2=AA*COS(A*PI/180)-SQR((2*CC*COS(A*PI/180))^2-4*(CC*CC-AA*AA))/2
1470 IF BB1 AND BB2>0 THEN 1940
1480 C=SIN(A*PI/180)
1490 C=C/SQR(1-C*C)
1500 C=CC*C/AA
1510 C=ATN(C)
1520 IF SQR(AA*AA+BB1*BB1-2*AA*BB1*COS(C))<(CC-.05) THEN C=PI-C
1530 C=C*180/PI
1540 B=180-(A+C)
1550 RETURN
1560 IF C=0 THEN 1940
1570 BB1=AA*COS(C*PI/180)+SQR((2*AA*COS(C*PI/180))^2-4*(AA*AA-CC*CC))/2
1580 BB2=AA*COS(C*PI/180)-SQR((2*AA*COS(C*PI/180))^2-4*(AA*AA-CC*CC))/2
1590 IF BB1 AND BB2>0 THEN 1940
1600 A=SIN(C*PI/180)
1610 A=AA*A/CC
1620 A=A/SQR(1-A*A)
1630 A=ATN(A)
1640 IF SQR(BB1*BB1+CC*CC-2*CC*BB1*COS(A))<(AA-.05) THEN A=PI-A
1650 A=A*180/PI:BB=BB1
1660 B=180-(A+C)
1670 RETURN
1680 IF A=0 THEN 1800
1690 CC1=BB*COS(A*PI/180)+SQR((2*BB*COS(A*PI/180))^2-4*(BB*BB-AA*AA))/2
1700 CC2=BB*COS(A*PI/180)-SQR((2*BB*COS(A*PI/180))^2-4*(BB*BB-AA*AA))/2
1710 IF CC1 AND CC2>0 THEN 1940
1720  B=SIN(B*PI/180)
1730 B=BB*B/AA
1740 B=B/SQR(1-B*B)
1750 B=ATN(B)
1760 IF SQR(AA*AA+CC1*CC1-2*CC1*AA*COS(B))<(BB-.05) THEN B=PI-B
1770 B=B*180/PI:CC=CC1
1780 C=180-(A+B)
1790 RETURN
1800 IF B=0 THEN 1940
1810 CC1=AA*COS(B*PI/180)+SQR((2*AA*COS(B*PI/180))^2-4*(AA*AA-BB*BB))/2
1820 CC2=AA*COS(B*PI/180)-SQR((2*AA*COS(B*PI/180))^2-4*(AA*AA-BB*BB))/2
1830 IF CC1 AND CC2>0 THEN 1940
1840 A=SIN(B*PI/180)
1850 A=AA*A/BB
1860 A=A/SQR(1-A*A)
1870 A=ATN(A)
1880 IF SQR(BB*BB+CC1*CC1-2*CC1*BB*COS(A))<(AA-.05) THEN A=PI-A
1890 A=A*180/PI:CC=CC1
1900 C=180-(A+B)
1910 RETURN
1920 ?"GIVEN ONE SIDE ONLY, MUST HAVE AT LEAST TWO ANGLES"
1930 STOP
1940 ?"NO SINGLE SOLUTION"
1950 STOP
1960 BB=AA*SIN(B*PI/180)/SIN(A*PI/180)
2070 ?FN G(AA),FN G(BB),FN G(CC), FN F(A),FN F(B),FN F(C)
2080 ?:?:?" (SIDES ARE TO 3 D.P., ANGLES ARE TO 1 D.P.)":?:?:?
2090 RETURN
```

# 7. BIBLIOGRAPHY & REFERENCES

**Ahl**, D. (1975) *101 BASIC Computer Games*

**Alcock**, D. (1977) *Illustrating Basic* Cambridge University Press

**Ferguson**, A. (2004) A History of Programming Languages http://cs.brown.edu/ (accessed 27/1/2014)

**Green**, D. (2011) *History of BASIC Programming Language*

**Knapp**, S. (2004) *Back to BASICs 40 years later* VOX Dartmouth College Newspaper

**Kopnicky**, L. (2011a) *Vintage BASIC User's Guide 1.0.2*

**Kopnicky**, L. (2011b)

http://www.vintage-basic.net/downloads/Vintage_BASIC

(accessed 3/1/2014)

**Marconi**, A. History of BASIC. *History of the BASIC Programming Language* http://www.q7basic.org/(accessed 27/12/2013)

**Price**, E. (2012) *A Brief History of Small Basic* http://blogs.msdn.com/b/smallbasic accessed 27/1/2014

(1978) BASIC PROGRAMMING REFERENCE MANUAL *APPLESOFT II* Apple Computer Inc.

(2000) Microprocessor-based Computers. Block 2 Program development and the C language *T223 Technology: A Level 2 Course* The Open University

(1985) *The PCW8256 and PCW8512 User Guide* AMSOFT

## ABOUT THE AUTHOR

Initially educated at a secondary modern school, leaving with 3 'A' levels Peta Trigger went on to university to gain honours degrees in Mathematics, Education and Engineering Science and a post graduate degree in Educational Psychology. Peta continued her education at London University's Institute of Education where she eventually completed her Ph.D and Ed.D degrees in Mathematics and Engineering Science Education. Her research for the Ed.D involved the development of computer programs in teaching undergraduate engineering science.

She is 64 and has lived in Northampton for 17 years.

www.ingramcontent.com/pod-product-compliance
Lightning Source LLC
Chambersburg PA
CBHW061020050326
40689CB00012B/2693